The Unmapped Woman

The Unmapped Woman

Abegail Morley

Nine
Arches
Press

The Unmapped Woman
Abegail Morley

ISBN: 978-1-911027-91-1
eISBN: 978-1-911027-92-8

First published April 2020 by:

Nine Arches Press
Unit 14, Sir Frank Whittle Business Centre,
Great Central Way, Rugby.
CV21 3XH
United Kingdom

www.ninearchespress.com

Nine Arches Press is supported using public funding by Arts Council England.

Supported using public funding by
ARTS COUNCIL
ENGLAND

Where you used to be, there is a hole in the world,
which I find myself constantly walking around
in the daytime, and falling in at night.

– Edna St. Vincent Millay

Contents

III

I

Egg

I breathe into the lonely snow-lines on the scan,
tell you how to grow safely, how to throw
and catch a ball, how later, stronger, fleshed out,
you'll thrust up a hand in class before the question's asked,
then hush, hush yourself before bed.

I tell you about a lot of things: Clarice Cliff teapots,
Georgia O'Keefe, tiny relief etchings we're making,
you circled in me and I'm blistering in midday sun.
I tell you about kissing at swimming pools,
little black dresses, apologies and apologies.
I say, *Be stronger than me* and mean every word
and plait your long blonde hair in innocence,
which I regret. I say, *Feel safe with lullabies,
don't be scared of fairy tales*, but know you should be.

I say, *Opening an umbrella indoors is bad luck,
as are new shoes on tables, walking under ladders, black cats.*
I fail to tell you we all fall out of luck with luck.
When you fall out of it there will be a train whispering
a promise, a half-stepped-on pavement, a book's page
slicing your small forefinger as it turns the page
of the epic novel you'll never finish.

I tell you about cutting your hair short and suffering
the consequences, and about huge paintings by women
who've disappeared; I will speak of my perimeters,
the way I brush my hair, cathedral ceilings
and how they are painted. I tell you, when you exist,
you will be all of these things and so much more:
we'll write your spine in charcoal, your heart in ink.

Gravid

Not until after the front door slams shut
and absence sucks air from its cheeks
do the words in her head, packed tight
as if on postcards, unhook their ink.

She knows their sloping script by rote,
has read each one to the echo of her womb,
laid her palm on her belly as she read them
aloud. She said, *Cessation, cessation,*

second trimester, over like a chant as if
wood fairies found a loophole in time,
wound arms and legs from blades of grass,
tugged saplings for spines, wove slews

of apple blossom into hair. And for the heart –
she can barely breathe now – the heart comes
from the stunned corpse of a doe, bulged
like late-summer fruit. She heaves herself

across fields, rubs rain-creased dock leaves
on her left thigh, shuffles past cows
flogging milk into machines, breathing
slow-flung air in sharp plumes. For one

unbridled moment she thinks she can run
through buckled nettles, the barbed thickets
of brambles, straggle shoulder-high thistles
all the way down the lane and never

come back to her silent grey world. But she
remembers the locksmith, his dreamt-up
names for keys, how you can half-turn them
in the nuzzle of a lock and nothing will open.

The voices

It's not until each candle is snuffed, shrugs off
its stuttering light so spirals of smoke thin upwards
that the wreck of embers finally closes its eyes.

She pinches a hushed, warm stump between thumb
and wet finger, hears it wince like a swallowed tongue –
its silty phrase sticking to her fingertips. She wipes

two soot lines across each cheek as if arming herself
for battle and in the blackout fidgets in a high-backed chair
until stars shift above tree tops, lose themselves.

There's no squeal of hinges, slammed front door,
trampled feet across lino – just the back of a hand
ghosting from shadows as if sky suddenly fell.

Today voices riddle like woodworm, each larva
gleams, stretches to a long vowel that sounds
like whisky tumbling into a glass, the empty echo

of a spanner dropped in a cold garage.
She watches the window: the glass, not the view –
knows crossing beyond it is out of the question.

Expected

We all start in water – endure its fullness,
bellies hoarding each molecule,
the swell of its ocean windblown
for a thousand miles.

So when her tide breaks,
she's hauled from
the house with the knowledge
she's rupturing.

I brim mid-stride
on the uneven pavement, split our blood
for the first time. She watches me
glisten across tarmac,

takes her fulsome weight from the kerb
to the taxi, hopes to replenish
us both with a sack full of saline,
knows

she's not the right one
to receive the cuckoo-baby nestling
in the thud of her pelvic bones.

Imminent

You thicken in me in the hottest June for years.
A soft fist smudges the wall of my womb and at night,
when it is already too hot to sleep, I watch your
elbow soar like a sail and imagine you journeying
upstream, skin pinking at a confluence of rivers,
body uncertain, smirching the bank. You're waiting
for liberation, foetus shaping in liquid until you
come adrift on a crib-shaped island with the map
of life crumpled in the tiniest palm I can imagine.
I see you unroll its tide-worn edges years later,
when you've waded with my handmade limbs
through life's inky waters. I picture you with my
youthful face and in early morning light, hear
for the first time how you pronounce your name.

Ultrasound

Today my face revolves to a full moon on the scan.
You stroke the weight of me and I know you need two

hands now just to gather me in. I sense the thrum
of your voice oscillate through muscle and roar like a river

at its mouth, ready for the swell. I want you to hear me.
I don't yet know there's only two months left with you,

I don't know it is not a love that lasts a lifetime.
Or a shared one. I hear that voice of yours

in my underworld through all your sleepless nights
and don't know that all the things you say aren't just to me.

I don't yet know, nuzzled here in the very centre of you
that I won't hear your voice on the other side.

Daughter bulb

You grow in me. I call you petal
and your name buds on my tongue at night.
We're spooned in sleep, skin on skin
and I purr lullabies from sap-filled lips until
your limbs purl like newly-woken shoots:
fresh leaves wait for nursing, suckling.

I name you Lily, and in the bulb of my belly
the veins of your body knit together
and you sleepwalk inside me,
make tiny footprints in blurred dreams,
trail my spine with satin feet as if you
own each and every inch of me. I don't know
which one of us is the honey, which the bee,
or who has the nectar we drink so deeply.

Lorn

I carry you to full term, daughter; know the
twitch of limbs, the tick of your cartilage,

the back road of each bone. We have sat
in waiting-rooms together, been checked-out

when we checked-in. I held you in me as long
as I could. The scan is just our bruising.

You're rose-hipped in me and the din
of everything else is petrified on film.

You will have your moment in my ambition,
be unburnable. I know your eyes will be green.

This is the first child I will make. The next one
I will keep because I can. You are the one

I have to let go down B-roads, down rickety lanes,
down tracks I cannot travel.

I know you'll swab my cells from yours,
but the hush of my blood will find you

as night's dull ache moans on tarmac
outside your bedroom window.

Given up

I could've thrust my legs to womb's stretch point,
to where elbows reached membrane, to where
no room's left for anywhere else to be
under this unreal red sky. I should've shifted new flesh

cell by cell as it grew, unheld breath, squealed
in my latched chamber, just to feel echoes of myself
ripple back through fluid. I could've been more
than life in liquid, crippled in womb's first flush –

a mistake that even gin, bathwater and a single-pointed
needle couldn't puncture. She has the exit wounds,
carmine, clamped wide for my departure – even numbed,
she felt the insult of my last small kick.

Given up II

She's unborn, eyes sealed, invisible stars
in an amniotic universe. She pauses for fire,

oxygen, the piston of birth, brutal takeover
of life. Her numb self hangs unheld,

fibulae carefully laid in darkness –
the wrong child in the wrong place.

A winter bulb; bruised root; pomegranate
seed throbbing. Each word I speak worries

us both, disappoints. She rocks underwater,
skull hardening – an unplucked knot.

Baby

Today I'm told to do a lap
of the ward and you refuse to move.
I tell them this, but they do not waver.
It's as if the anaesthetic's already kicked in
and I'm counting snowflakes down
from ten and wondering
in what pattern you will fall.

This is our secret, *Baby*, and as I say this
I know you'll never know it. You are thawing,
bones milky, heart valve shunting
warmth through mist. Somewhere in me
you're somersaulting in a driven wind
towards the exit, and water is rising.

I imagine your little chin begging
to be held up, know there's an undercurrent,
some women will buckle at the knee,
abandon their babies,
leave them like milk on a doorstep.

Baby, I want to give you more
than this snapshot of your unborn self
cradled in snow's blanket on the sonographer's scan.
I want to dig a hollow
for your fat baby legs to stagger through.
I want to be there for you when the thaw comes.

Sweetheart

Of all the babies, I am this one.
The Sunday one,
the late in the day one,
the corner-shop, convenience store
bagged one, the end of the week
couldn't keep one.

I'm the weight of three bags of sugar
and you carried me that long
hot summer hidden from sunlight
in the bulk of your belly –
but couldn't hide me when I was ripe.

You were fruited for months
and in some hospital bed, clinical
and white, a little red secret
dropped into the midwife's hands
like rain itself and my thirsty mouth
screamed when your pulse unplugged
itself from mine.

Seed

I know you are pocket-small, an ounce of flour,
a quiet girl sifting herself tooth and nail through
tiny mesh, as if dying by degrees. I count you
by single grains until your emptiness blooms,
reappears as an arm, then a leg, until
your whole being forms in my re-imagining.

When you left, sterilised, my gown was loosened;
its patterned fabric flowers puckered their small mouths,
tiny forget-me-nots wilted. I left when you were singing
in your beautiful sleep. I left you by the window
and the woman on the radio was talking about funerals
and caskets, and said she had a remedy for loss;
It's all to do with eggs, she said.

The sun was beating down, grass browning,
and I knew by each increment I was losing you.
Imagine if it was colder, the kind of cold
that leaves lakes stoppered by ice – it would be like
diving into someone else's sorrow. Suddenly
it is painfully enticing to push my body through glass.

For remembrance

I love my chosen names; zip and unzip them from my neck
as if I can reveal two bodies simultaneously, let down
a sheath of blonde hair only I can clamber up. I think

of you, mother, registering my birth. The awkward pen
slipping your grip, the silence of the page fumbling
beneath black ink, that radio song in the back of your mind,

heady as Jasmine. I think of you moisturising your belly
and your soap-scrubbed body and the woman who
imagined her world would not be this. I think of you

with your sawn-off tongue so you wouldn't tell,
breasts stoked with milk, and I know how hard it is for you
to let me go, when I've kicked and kicked to see daylight.

Preserve

Yesterday I took a knife, hulled strawberries,
cut them in half, boiled hard in the preserving pan,
skimmed off scum, mastered the art of waiting:

dipped spoons into sugar to feel its grains,
sterilised jars, warmed them in the oven, poured
boiling jelly – too soon. Maybe it was all too soon for you.

I remember steam in the kitchen, the unendurable heat,
the blurred lettering on jars naming where they came from,
how the flame buckled when I opened the door.

I remember you as if it was yesterday, how you'd held
a note in your fist as if begging for forgiveness,
and I know your eyes were closed when you didn't write it,

and I know, just lying on the floor with the late-sun beating in
I could watch your foetal flutters shadow themselves
all day long and I could account for each and every breath

you may or may not have made. And I remember it all
as if it was yesterday when minutes bleated and you put
your lovely mouth up against the world and everyone listened.

Cutting the cord

I take this first birth, this cavern of a scan,
this black and white photo stuck

to the fridge door, its grainy hollow throbbing
like a pulse. I take this first birth

on a stroll down the well-after-dark backstreets
of this small town, recall our memories,

common language, think how one day our faces
might press nose-to-nose outside the windows

of this shut-tight shop as it coughs limp light
over out-of-date stock. I take this first birth

past the women on the crossing who clutch fast
to their children's hands with fingers that

stroked foreheads and wrists and guided lips.
I take this first birth, this not-yet-ready-birth,

this empty, unplugged, dead season of the year,
to its own thin air, skin's edge, beginnings,

and let its tiny unformed throat, like oil-thick sea,
tell me where to take it, tell me where home is.

Dear Baby

At the end of this there's... at the end... there is.
I feel your noisy dreams ripple through me.
I whisper, *Am I there with you?* Sometimes I taste you,
roll your name across my tongue, silently savour
each syllable for as long as I can, feel your beautiful hurt
each time my lips press together.

At the end of this there's morning light, virgin skin,
a newness so soft we're all afraid we'll break it.
I break it – feel the stab of my *accident* over and over
as they take you from me, and you blur into the distance,
backsliding from my life. I wonder,

when they slip the hospital tag around your miracle ankle,
if they will say your name aloud so the whole ward hears
and people clap like heavy rain and someone,
just one person, holds you to their body so tight
it's like a whole night's rain is pooling in their arms.

II

Playing fields

We come to look at the bones.
Your hand fumbles mine, palm sticky,
wax crayon-coated. He lures us somehow,
leads us to the field's edge, pokes with a stick, shouts:
See there. No there. We search the earth
to see the dead man's corpse, how his skull
leaks worms, larvae burrow in sockets,
beetles, black as currants, shuttle themselves
click-clicking over shins and elbows.

He spits in his palm, makes me spit in mine,
then shake. I drop yours to do it. It's the hottest
day of the holidays – you shiver,
chapped bottom lip hanging like a gash.
You stuff in your thumb.
I smell the barley; hear it crack in the heat.

Cutting ties

Time, he says, is just a line
from beginning to end,
a sheared strand of string
dangling limply from
an outstretched hand.

I try to tell him that string
runs from end to end
and has no beginning, but
now he speaks of knots
and journeys and how

we unravel ourselves from
each other. I'm threadbare,
as if I've plucked holes
in myself since my beginnings
looped. He is whole; yards

of twine spool from him,
reminds me of a biology class,
a gash of intestines, scalpel –
no start or finish line.
It doesn't matter how carefully

you pick or unpick time,
you bruise yourself to the crypt
of your bones, orphan emotions
from your core so they unpack
themselves minute by minute

in some place you'd never
willingly go, but go tonight.
Maybe I shouldn't carry
scissors or a knife in my bag.
Maybe I shouldn't carry time.

Past love

Into the darkness they go, the wise and the lovely
  – Edna St. Vincent Millay

He tells me how planets orbit each other, offers five
long-stemmed roses, red-faced, shuffles from one foot
to the other. He speaks of constellations, particles,
Telstars, ends up asking in a snatched speech, *What is*

the meaning of life? I wonder if now's a good time
to tell him about you, but talk instead about the rising star
of Orion, which I know nothing about, and on a scale of
one-to-ten am hovering around three in my knowledge of the cosmos.

I hope he'll ask again, some time when I'm ready,
but he moves effortlessly forward and the blooms of two roses
fall like stardust, soundlessly, like you did, when somehow
your life was sucked, ever so gently, from your lungs.

When I held you, there was no noise from this galaxy
or another or another, and we spent that night wondering
how the sun lit only other people, and how breathless
the universe can be when you need air the most.

Last night

Nothing happens like winter. Not even
the clock's slow tick next to your hospital bed
can deaden like snow. Its long, sleek crucifix hands
still drag themselves as if through drifts, ice's fog,
to carve time's unsteady voice
in this half-darkened ward, on this sterile night.

I walk into a whirl of flakes, mouth wide as a hole
chipped through ice so I can fish and feed you.
I think I've been an Inuit at some time past,
culled a seal, pulled its pelt from shoulder
to cheek just to keep warm. I check on my children,
burrowed in furs, every hour of their waking.
When they're asleep I still pinch and poke them
with an ungloved forefinger and thumb,
know I love them more than time itself –
know time isn't forever, that it can melt
any day now and I'll lose myself in a river of you,
slide behind in slippers of meltwater.
You breathe frost on the clock's face. And it stops.
My veins are blurred with cold, skin just a mist in air.
Is it you who is leaving my touch?
I can't take my hands from you, though the nurse tugs.
I can't take the way you are thawing
when I've shut the blinds to keep out morning's light.

Where you used to be

Your shape is here again, slides into your chair,
as if every night you're fastened to cushions,

stripping feathers from your wings like silence.
I flick the TV – channel by channel – until shadows

reveal how you launch for flight, but never leave –
each skinned wing aloft with nowhere to go.

When I go, I'll unmap myself from this world,
tug pins like stitches, watch them stretch and snap.

Green light

He thinks it's strange that nothing's ever felt
quite like this. We're wearing armistice
poppies on our lapels, red-hulled hearts beating

like late-fledged birds caught in autumn's frost.
My numb lips hardly move; it's as if he's
suddenly invented time and we walk out of stride

down wide Exeter pavements, trundle
hand in hand as though passing a lit torch
to a couple heaped in winter coats, convinced

love belongs to them. He shows me the colour
of the road, how at night it lights up green
and as far as he knows nobody else has seen it.

The Quick

I wish you hadn't told me how you saw a magpie
from your window jab at a starling's head,

how you ran downstairs, halted to slip on shoes,
got there too late and saw it unhinge each tiny eye

from its slick socket. I wish, when you saw it,
you'd run barefoot across gravel kicking your legs

until the unbroken hatchling caught its breath,
heart soft-pedalled inside its newly-woken chest.

This morning my sister found four plump feathers
curled on the doorstep, gathered them, gave one

to each saying it's a sign from you, how we're not
forgotten. I watch a hawk circling and know

its stomach is full of newly-whispering dead,
and the blood rising on its beak is still warm.

Fire ants

And they don't die, they just keep spooling
like breath and even when the path is swept free
of soil they still pool in damp patches. You instruct me
to stamp on them, and not to think so much,
but I watch the rivulets pour, their rapid-cool bodies
like endless traffic serpentining cracks, bridging gaps
in the earth until next door's dog starts howling as it never
has before and I know that something terrible
has happened over the fence. People are dropping
glasses, cutlery, running across the lawn, and paper plates
fall soundlessly, as if to blend in with the grass and sky
that have waited quietly all day and remain unsurprised
when the woman, next door, does what she did.

And earlier when we were clearing the patio, you hosed
me down as a joke, and the water spewed over the wisteria
and the woman next door shouted because they had
tablecloths laid out and a little awning, and you showed
me scribbles in your notebook, mocked "her next door",
ran your fingers across a smeared page of words,
said, *Things can be lost for ever.* Then shrugged
as if it didn't really matter. We are playing that game
you do with a hose, when each spurt of water held back
by the thumb is a word you'd like to say, or a curse,
and you're aiming at next door's fence, covering and
uncovering the hose with your thumb and I'm laughing
because it sounds like Morse code, and I am laughing
because I am deciphering its meaning and you're falling
backwards into the magnolia bush, as if in slow motion,
and the hose is unfurling into a magnificent plume
and the woman next door is shouting.

But all we want to do is sort out the ants. Last year a trail
of them made their way inside the house, ran around the
edges of the carpet right past the TV, so today we're here,
sentries at our posts, kettle in my hand, brush in yours.
And I am still holding it, when everyone next door has
dropped everything they are holding, and they're running
to the patio doors and something is happening, and then
there is shrieking, and you're poking me in the ribs
and I let the kettle fall, don't hear it crash on the patio,
don't feel the lick of boiling water on my legs, don't
know they can run that fast to the front door, to
next door. When I hold her I know she's already dead,
and I watch an ant crawl across my shoulder, down
my arm, and I hang on to her because she once told me,
just after we moved in, that she'd rather die alone,
and now a whole colony of relatives are picking
their way through the doors and I can't keep them back.

Snapshot on the beach

I slip my whole self
into his camera click

duck in and out of film,
with each tick and whirr.

He zooms in on my neck
where five shells hang empty,

circle my throat,
ululate as I swallow.

My own seawall is lined
with mussels that creak

in the colour of midnight.

I stumble to stand upright
in soft pillows of sand,

his camera purring,
shrinking sunlight on water

to the *keow, keow* of gulls –
their screech lilting waves

to a frightened lisp.
In the darkroom later, he sinks

my body in the stop bath,
careful not to dip his hands in

too far, too deep.

Exposure

What if, when he takes it
I slide blade-like towards him
as if to cut myself from paper
before I develop, or worse still
am allergic to acetic acid.

What if he unravels its spool,
sleeves rolled to elbows
and the tiny image of me keels
like a dragonfly over the stop bath,
all wings and light from shivs.

What if I float in this liquid,
skinny-dip in its swell,
lose myself in its silver.
What if I skate across its surface
as if I don't give a damn.

Losing it

There's a time when a woman will forget her own name,
it can't trickle through an hourglass, trip off her tongue.

If she leaves it too long it can't peel from reluctant light,
heal into silver keloid scars, and the passerby who looks

directly into her eyes will see her well of silence.
It can't smell of the river where it walked, blackberries

jamming in a pan, the years of blindness to his faults.
It can't sing out of doors, rush to a window, disappear

each night to regain itself in the dawn, doesn't dream
in black and white, think of old films, rewrite great novels

in freehand. Its meaning is just gaps in text, white paper,
lengths of unbundled cotton drying in the sun. But in her

heavy-handed unfamiliar voice, its echo grips the seams,
its stillness as quick as light or a sleight of hand.

Still

I clamp mercury-filled teeth, imagine planets clattering
inside a shut-tight mouth – I'm the Milky Way
arching in darkness. Outside my body

women scrub until the smell of sour milk clings
to fabric, wallpaper, full-length striped curtains
smothering windows on the south side of the house.

Inside, I'm quicksand, ice melting, an undecided
summer's day. I swallow myself in a blether of words.
They whittle me like I'm unfallen snow.

Neap tide

Someone told me children are plentiful, can be collected
like shells. I imagine their beach; a shelf of fragments,
I pile them high and underline my act in sand

so the sea folds in and fills the gaps. I hoe a trench so water
scarifies sand, tilts on the leeside and your net fills itself
with weed and somewhere in it something moves.

I watch you dance in sunlight, toss your curls and limbs
until every bit of you aches, and I watch how you weigh the wind
on chapped lips, bear its salted chafe on scabbed knees.

Sometimes I only seem to watch your pain outlined
by the headland, windbreakers, the extremities of a rockpool.
None of this makes you any greater, exist.

I find a stretch of sea, driftwood, an old coil of rope
and stack it up, so you can play with it later,

when the tide draws out.

Shell

When she raises it, it's weightless as a butterfly's wing,
a wren's egg that's lost its nestling. She carries it in anyway,

aloft (for drama) and the bare floor beneath her feet
creaks in sympathy as if she pulls a knotted whorl

from each plank's hemming stitch. I shake it out of her grasp
without caution, death no longer makes me shudder.

I let her clatter on the stairs like erratic shingle settling
on the shore, know sometime soon we'll sit

and talk it through. I watch as she self-seeds herself in mirrors.
My uncremated twin, just a finger-pull away, is crying now.

I know she's curling into a tiny comb, pulling in her limbs,
her head – just waiting to disappear in wax and pollen.

The Promotion of Forgetting

If he cannot silence her absolutely, he tries to make sure no one listens.
  – Judith Lewis Herman

I chronicle time, study how light bends the hands
of his watch, how they cut through chambered rivers of sleep,
find themselves paddling back, exhausted. Unaware,
each resistant tick assigns itself to movement, locking
eyes, limbs – I'm stuck-shut, know his watch face

holds mine in its mock-gilt grin, tells me I'm sick
with the spirit of the dead. Yet I shift my weight,
cough my name, unpeel his shabby story with just
one breath. I can tug a whole fish bone from my throat
as a party-piece if I want. I'm surprised by someone

who holds my gullet shut, with just one clench.
I don't strain for air, but check my skin for prints,
know there are far too many to be wiped clean.
He walks now, unmistakably him, gathers those seconds
close. I'm not even cold when he devises his lies.

On keeping yourself whole and giving nothing away

As soon as the dimming happens and sun spins itself
behind houses, she goes to the front window,

palms on sill's lip. Its glossy coat under each finger's pad
comforts something in her as if her twin slips his hand

in hers and their young knuckles touch again. She
remembers him cleaving bark, penknife daring sap,

whittling twigs to resemble people, arms akimbo
like they'd been shot. Later it's not this she recalls

as she pours wine into an already sullied glass, it's the man
down the street, black-maned, who liked to play

boy-soldiers, would hold her too tight, say he could sniff
out a girl at twenty paces, on a good night.

This is his good night, twisting her arm with two hands
as if wrenching a jar's stiff lid from glass.

Fished

It's not true that life is one damn thing after
another; it is one damn thing over and over
  – Edna St. Vincent Millay

Lastly, and this is what he really means to say –
it doesn't help that it's pissing down and grey skies
withdraw with the hardness of rock, and I have to
listen to him with a cardiologist's expert ear –
Lastly, he says, then somehow moves time on,

maps out my flesh with a black ballpoint pen
makes me an island he's sick of navigating,
thighs creased together, air-tight, draws lines
down each, presses too hard and somewhere
in the nuzzle of sheets, I know I'm the Atlantic,

or maybe a lesser sea, just water, barnacles,
sand-shadowed pools. Tide swells under my knees
and I know he's a fisherman splitting clams,
resting on haunches so knife's curve is deep
and each leg drifts like fog over oceans.

Last words

That night, two hours after, in a narrow bed
in a cheap hotel, time reverses like egrets

retreating ungainly into the egg's globe.
Tissue crawls, unhealed wounds repair

under a dim 40 Watt bulb, flesh clings
to calcite, shell's splinters heal.

I take your words, crack each one, release
yolk from white, hide them until my pockets

burst with sunbeams or fat yellow buttons
purled to fabric. I know you want them back,

to somehow hatch them, crack them open
catch each one, hold them captive.

The Library of Broken People

is catalogued by injury: the fractured;
the ruined from hunger; the raped;

the hammered shut. Some are clumped
together as "lost souls"; only the librarian

can retrieve those. There's no ABC to damage,
they litter the alphabet ad hoc. If you browse

the catalogue they give their injuries, lay
themselves flat. Last week two girls displayed

their abdomens to a first-year student –
bickered over abuse, spoke of neglect,

said life's an unworkable toy. Other victims
are quieter, don't talk so much, even when

the library's shut. They drop to the back
of the index, all seal pup-eyed, skittering

at the slightest flex. I survive amongst them,
wear a long jumper, drag sleeves down wrists.

III

A Rough Guide to Grief: after reading the leaflet

There's a softness to loss, how it collapses in your palm,
spills down your life-line with a stubborn slowness.

It writhes in spare rooms where radiators are wrenched shut,
guests stripped from beds – washed, folded, put away.

In languid afternoons it vanishes only to reappear
in sun-trapped dust, gleam like a glassy far-off sea.

At night, roused by wind, its footsteps patter across
floors that can't groan under weightlessness,

quail as each measured step lays itself flat on oak.
This morning I hear it champ its teeth, almost hiss

its *Hello*, and under bedsheets my labouring heart
slaps beat after beat as if tame diurnal tides surge

against the latch of lung's cavity, rattle its lock.
Last night I yanked it shut so it couldn't clamber in,

but discover loss nestled against tendons, slipping sea's
neck, floating in slack water, haltingly turning home.

Accidental

I will touch a hundred flowers and not pick one
  – Edna St. Vincent Millay

Yesterday I forgot you entirely –
well almost.
I forgot how you died at least, and today
I realise I might have, in error,
sliced the roots of the rose you loved,
and in the low-setting sun can almost
forgive myself. But not quite.

I know you flinch like stopped sea
pooling itself like a myth in the cold
and February's naked air slowly realises
and is struck by you jumping
from a quiet cliff, mid-week,
when everything is supposed to be ordinary.

Barometer

After the funeral, words
were deadpan, slipped
down my throat like gullied-rain.
Today the weather's changed,
someone's placed graph paper
against the pane, plotted the day –
it peaks around ten.

I snake out of sheets,
abandon them like a swag of leaves,
move across the room
with the slow precision
of newly-oiled machinery.

Not Being

The sun has cleaved its way in,
its fists full of fire, scattering throbs
of unpocketed light. I look at myself:
my hands, scorched fingers, palms.

I wait for melancholy to wake,
snared like a hack of crow
at the back of my throat.
I wait to weigh its grief at daybreak,

surrender its pear-shaped lungs
to the snuff of night.

Grief: Stage 1

The reality is that you will grieve forever
– Elisabeth Kübler-Ross

In this dark-bellied night even my hands are strangers,
dragging back curtains so I can see if
one light down the entire street is awake with me.

Clouds slouch on each other not knowing the sky's
at breaking point too. Now's the time,
in night's trap to be art-model still,

allow light to fall on my throat, pick its way
down the fall and rise of ribs, ascend each,
desperate for the soft siren of descent.

Grief: Stage 2

My hands are thick with it, hairline bleeds
with its stench – I rub until I'm stippled red,
its unslaked need soused by water's weight.

I lose every language there ever was in the black wire
between throat and lungs; I'm belljarred, mute,
curled at the end of a deliberate breath, warm in its mist.

From the floor I can see the thumb-top of the stairs
hear the broken song of your footsteps in the passage.
Cannot call your name, cannot call, cannot.

The hollowing of the empty place

It was just that I didn't know why I wanted to go on.

– Kay Redfield Jamison

Don't be surprised when she stares you out
in amber-thin light, repeats herself,
as if counting valves and ventricles, rolling over
each muscle in slow motion, each time she ends up
in A & E, incubated, trolley-moved at dawn to AAU.

She doesn't have a story of tanks, knee-capping,
an A-Z of horrors that keep her awake. She has this.
She has this every day and some days it's better
and she shapes crushed lips, shoals vowels,
each nubbin a stuttered word. She remembers the sky,
its lack of blue, every sentence he said,
and the way he planted a word in her mouth
to germinate after he'd gone.

On having enough messages from the dead

Your name is paperweighted to my tongue.
Each time I try to lift it, it bangs to the floor
of my mouth, bulky as a sandbag,
or an iron girder from that old advert.
Your name trundles on wheels, heavy
in its criss-crossing skids, but like a glass
memory is always reflecting something else.

I decide to pin your name to the noticeboard,
stick another to the fridge with a magnet,
to loosen you from me. This morning I find
they've dived off, parachuted down
and are hissing on an unwashed floor –
paper sun-torn, unbearable to touch.
I watch ink vacate itself from the present.

Grief: Stage 3

I can't drown in my demons, they know how to swim.

– Fish, Malia, Sykes

By daylight I'm fish-hooked, raw limbed,
washed-up loss in every crevice of my body
from skull to toe, burrows deep, hides itself in marrow.
I've been night-fishing in my dreams, scaled

water's lip on moonlit seas, the soles of my feet
now blue. You ask how I've harboured here,
run ashore when wind dropped two days ago,
spinnaker fell flat on deck. Your question ripples,

undresses – naked sounds, thin as sprats,
swim from you, as if an undercurrent cracks the boom
of your voice and the propped-up sky crumples
around me. I watch your mouth move like sails

hoisted up and down, the twitch of muscle
around your eyes, a tail's flick. I sleepwalk,
squint in your face, pupils wide open –
I think you see fishermen in them, hauling nets,

capturing night. You find me later, crouched
in a corner, skimming water in rock pools,
looking for a trophy, a reason to be here.

Bereavement

I inhale again and something in my unclaimed body
shifts as if a folding chair, shoved away at summer's end,
is left to poke around in ageing cobwebs.

I listen to the next exhale winch each fictional phrase
from its lexicon, let the silt of its words pour open.
Tonight, he calls loss from sky's bleak places

and I plunge my hands into kitchen's iced water
just to know how it feels to be dead,
to know how to unfeel. I wait in the *hintergrund*,

voice disappearing in the fingerholes of the sweater
I can't quite bear to take off because each stitch yearns
for the next and the next and there's no more next to give.

Woods' End

I walk as far as the woods, knowing I'll lose myself quite easily
in its hush of winter. The skinny fox that bolts from its panic
shifts twigs from its labyrinth of a den, makes me go quiet,
almost forget why I'm here. I take night in my stride, collect
dogwood, drifting days, keep my own handprints in the pockets
of my dressing-gown so I won't be lonely in my slow creep to you.

Sometimes it feels as if I'm coming back to you; you're in the bark
of every tree, knotted in its whorl of rings like a whole wall of snow
has packed you in and you're road-mapping your veins in sap
and the gaps in between are empty branches I trail through.

When trees are wintered they stop sharing their tales,
bare as a handless glove when the curl of left and right isn't
straightened by the bones of fingers. Tonight, in the forest
each leaf's a skull and I pick through its tiny teeth as if playing
Truth or Dare and expect you to pull yourself from the sea,
hang your clothes on low branches so tomorrow they'll dry
as if nothing has happened. You don't do that. There are no trees
where you fell, just cliffs that ricocheted your body,

picked your spine until my memory of you loosens its grip. My
tight-lipped face can only imagine the frozen figure of you hurtling
mid-air as if you're thinking you can run further than cliff's edge,
as if dawn will swallow you up and you'll be nose-to-nose
with a sea that extends its tongue to the very edges of its mouth,
but barely knows your name.

I take your fall home in your van and we drive like strangers
in our inescapable hill-starts, park you in a garage that's too small
to contain you. And I wait for you to settle, hear a whiff of music
split the air in the house. And I say to you, *I hate that you did that.*
I am sorry you did. And you nod and put out your hand.

Grief: Stage 4

I'm feverish. The moon tilts my head, presses
madness to my mouth. I swallow its toxic mistletoe,
warm Jerusalem berries, sun-sapped yew seeds.
Sheltered under my tongue a whole string of rosary beads
open and close their eyes like starlight
in a Hebridean winter.

Earlier you ransacked every inch
of the house, thrust your voice like a skean
into each room, slashed our curtains into strips
to bind our lesions with bolts of cotton.
Before that, you'd carefully traced
where my heart beats routinely under skin.

Small Voice

If you knew me at all, you'd know
I'm experimenting with these words,
tongue clucking against cheeks
trying to comfort them in the wound
of my mouth. But they're wading
deep water, heaving their tiny bodies,
dormouse, goldfinch, moth,
hearts bumping in unbelievably small chests.
Even the moth, in its shuffling
through blankets, fits its small wings
in to our lives. If you knew me
you'd take a few of my words,
jot them down like we used to
next to the phone, in case, just in case.
Fighting with you is like unsinging
and if you knew me you'd realise
it's the space between words
you need to hear. It's like stepping on
egg shells, stones across rivers,
daisies chasing roots over lawns that stretch
the full length of summer. If you knew me
at all, you'd forgive this.

Grief: Stage 5

I give my wrist because it is the thinnest thing I own,
because sometimes, most times, bones are all we can give.
Sometimes in circumstances like these hallucinations
are so clear I swear it is today, or maybe yesterday they happened
in full colour. Piccadilly's lights are still on full blast, the whole
of Blackpool's illuminations firing bright behind my eyes.

Today you say that's not it, tell me not to mourn my past
and live in the present. I wade through it knee-deep,
travel in slow motion. I call back to you
to tell me where to tread, how hard, how soft,
but in the wilderness my feet rot in the wrong soil, fibrous.

Sing that

There was a backward glance,
sleet falling on feathers,
spew of claws, a chitter of birdsong.
I can say it is poetic, or I can tell you what happened.

Bear with me. I can take nature,
let wind whip our faces in the low draw of your throat;
I can exist in slow air, watch it leech from you,

until I shrink myself like a self-wound because I listened
to how you loved me and, in the shock of grey rain,
in your studio flat, you emptied the entire room
and left.

End

Forget you. The ash of bone. The uncradled
heart, leaky valve long scorched. Forget
the unthinking arm that fell on my shoulder,
those times we crossed the M6 flyover
and you drove with one hand on the wheel
and I'd change gear, rather badly. Forget
the mix-tape, its erratic path through
teenage years, the growing up, beers, larking
about on bridges and piers and dancing
all night in the Zap Club. Forget the sea
and its snub-nosed wall, the hiss of shingle
on sand, the plans we made at 2am
to be bruised by life. Forget the headlamps
dimming on the Downs, the uphill walks,
the drinks in the Nelson, Trafalgar Street,
the way your heart beat. And beat. Remember
the dull ring of my doorbell, the slight tap
on glass, the way my stomach flipped when
I knew you were there, before you arrived.
Remember what longing means, the thick taste
of Milky Bars for breakfast, the crack of your elbow
broken on the stairs at 4am, the thud of your step
across floorboards. Remember how in that crowd
we found each other's silence, feathered it out,
knowing we might make it from friends to lovers
and friends again. Remember how we felt that night
when we each held our breaths, met under
an invisible sky. Remember how we said
when you died, I'd try to forget.

Acknowledgements

Many thanks to the editors of the following magazines in which some of these poems first appeared, sometimes in previous versions:

Agenda; Arfur; Atrium; Biot; Cake; The Bookends Review; Coast to Coast to Coast; The Frogmore Press; The Interpreter's House; Ink, Sweat and Tears; London Grip; The Lonely Crowd; Magma; The Moth; Poetry Birmingham Literary Journal; Poetry Salzburg Review; Prole; The Rialto; Riggwelter; Skylark Review; Shearsman and *Truth Anthology*, Tell Tale Press (2017). *Given up II* first appeared in *In the Curator's Hands*, Indigo Dreams Publishing, (2017).